CYBER SECURITY CERTIFICATIONS FOR BEGINNERS

Your Comprehensive Guide into the World of Cyber Security Certifications

Taimur Ijlal

About this book

This edition was published in **August 2023**

I have kept it as up-to-date as possible with the latest certifications and trends in Cybersecurity. However, the rapid rate at which tech evolves means that I will regularly update this book whenever any significant change happens.

Copyright © 2023 Taimur Ijlal

DEDICATION

This book is dedicated to my son and two daughters, who bring me so much joy. My wife, who regularly pushes me to take on new challenges and risks to better myself. My parents raised me to be the person I am today and never let me feel that I could not achieve what I set my mind to.

Thanks to all the people who watch my YouTube Channel, **"Cloud Security Guy,"** and appreciate all the comments/feedback I receive

Lastly, THANK YOU for purchasing this book, and I hope it gives you tangible advice on how to get that Cybersecurity Certification you have been dreaming about!

Taimur Ijlal

DEDICATION

This book is dedicated to my son and two daughters, who bring me so much joy. My wife, who regularly pushes me to take on new challenges and risks to better myself. My parents raised me to be the person I am today and never let me feel that I could not achieve what I set my mind to.

Thanks to all the people who watch my YouTube Channel, **"Cloud Security Guy,"** and appreciate all the comments/feedback I receive

Lastly, THANK YOU for purchasing this book, and I hope it gives you tangible advice on how to get that Cybersecurity Certification you have been dreaming about!

Taimur Ijlal

ABOUT THE AUTHOR

Taimur Ijlal is a multi-award-winning information security leader with over two decades of international experience in cyber-security and IT risk management in the fin-tech industry. For his contributions to the industry, he won a few awards here and there, such as CISO of the Year, CISO Top 30, CISO Top 50, and Most Outstanding Security Team.

He served as the Head of Information Security for several major companies, but his real passion is teaching and writing about cyber-security topics. He lives in the UK, where he moved with his family in 2021.

Taimur writes on Medium and has a YouTube channel, "Cloud Security Guy, " where he regularly posts about Cloud Security, Artificial Intelligence, and general cyber-security career advice.

He has published two books on AI Cybersecurity and Zero Trust, both of which can be purchased from Amazon. He also has several courses on Udemy and can be contacted on his LinkedIn profile for any consulting opportunities.

ABOUT THE BOOK

Cybersecurity Certifications!

Have you ever felt overwhelmed by the sheer number of cybersecurity certifications available in the market? You are not alone.

Your LinkedIn feed is probably filled with posts announcing to the world that "*I am pleased to inform you that I have passed XYZ exam*" along with a screenshot of that certification.

If you are new to Cybersecurity and the whole Certifications thing, it can all seem overwhelming!

Where to start? Which cert to pick? Which niche should I specialize in?

This is not a light decision as choosing the wrong certification can lead to wasted time and money hence it is essential to make the right choice. I was once in this position many years back and wished I had a guide that could tell me what certs I should go for and in what order. Hence the reason for writing this book.

The purpose behind this book is simple. This book will:
- Explain the WHYs and HOWs of Cybersecurity certifications
- Guide you towards the right cybersecurity certification based on your strengths
- Clarify common misconceptions about certifications
- Provide tips on acing certification exams
- Advise on next steps after certification

Before we proceed, it's important to note that this book does not teach you how to pass any specific certification. If you are interested in getting a shiny cert like the CISSP or CCSP then there are study guides already present for them.

No, this book is for people who want to know what certs they should attempt based on their strengths and career goals AND how to get them.

I wrote this book as a guide based on my own two decades plus experience in the industry. Cybersecurity is a MASSIVE field, and a person can easily get intimidated by the number of available options. This book is intended to make that journey easier and give you actionable advice on which path to take.

I have also given my own tips and advice on what to do AFTER getting certified and how to build your brand to get noticed and land that high-paying J-O-B.

Feedback is always appreciated

I always appreciate feedback, whether it is positive or negative, as that will help me improve as a writer and make better material. Please leave a review and let me know what you liked and where you think it can be improved.

1 – A Brief Introduction to Cybersecurity

Imagine a world where massive, room-filling computers were the norm and the Internet was still a revolutionary concept. That was the dawn of our digital era, and with it came the first "virus", forever changing the world of computers

Cybersecurity did not exist as a separate profession a few decades ago, at least not until the Internet came along and connected everyone. Suddenly we needed anti-viruses and something called "firewalls" to keep the bad guys out. Words like "phishing" and "identity theft" also became common. Then came the 21st century and a whole new era of "this is bad".

The new millennium witnessed a rapid escalation in cybersecurity threats as cybercriminals realized that there was more to this whole cybercrime thing than just irritating people, i.e., there was some serious money to be made

We saw the explosion of state-sponsored cyber warfare, massive data breaches, ransomware attacks, and the Internet of Things (IoT) botnets. This was a major turning point in the field of cybersecurity.

Cybersecurity in the Modern World

Fast forward to 2023, and cybersecurity has never been more crucial.

The World Economic Forum, in its Global Risks Report 2023 put Cybercrime at no. 8 on their Top 10 Risks stating:

"Alongside a rise in cybercrime, attempts to disrupt critical technology-enabled resources and services will become more common, with attacks anticipated against agriculture and water, financial systems, public security, transport, energy, and domestic, space-based, and undersea communication infrastructure. Technological risks are not solely limited to rogue actors. Sophisticated analysis of larger data sets will enable the misuse of personal information through legitimate legal mechanisms, weakening individual digital sovereignty and the right to privacy, even in well-regulated, democratic regimes."

Global Risks Report 2023

Top 10 Risks

"Please estimate the likely impact (severity) of the following
risks over a 2-year and 10-year period"

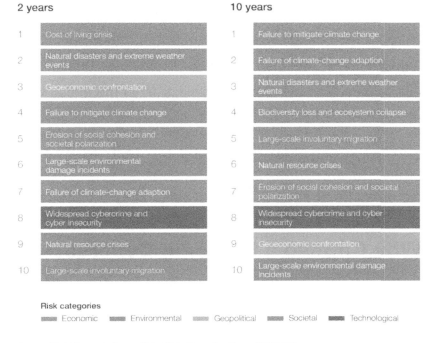

	2 years		10 years
1	Cost of living crisis	1	Failure to mitigate climate change
2	Natural disasters and extreme weather events	2	Failure of climate-change adaption
3	Geoeconomic confrontation	3	Natural disasters and extreme weather events
4	Failure to mitigate climate change	4	Biodiversity loss and ecosystem collapse
5	Erosion of social cohesion and societal polarization	5	Large-scale involuntary migration
6	Large-scale environmental damage incidents	6	Natural resource crises
7	Failure of climate-change adaption	7	Erosion of social cohesion and societal polarization
8	Widespread cybercrime and cyber insecurity	8	Widespread cybercrime and cyber insecurity
9	Natural resource crises	9	Geoeconomic confrontation
10	Large-scale involuntary migration	10	Large-scale environmental damage incidents

Risk categories

▬ Economic   ▬ Environmental   ▬ Geopolitical   ▬ Societal   ▬ Technological

Source: World Economic Forum, Global Risks Perception Survey 2022-2023

With an estimated 4.88 billion Internet users worldwide, and an untold number of devices, servers, and even toasters connected to the web, the digital world has become a playground for anyone with a keyboard and a less-than-ethical bent. With the advent of tools like ChatGPT, the situation has gotten even worse!

The digital world has become very scary but also fascinating.

The importance of cybersecurity in our current scenario cannot be overemphasized. It's not just about ensuring our systems are secure though that's a huge part.

It's about ensuring the integrity of our communication systems, safeguarding national security, protecting businesses and economies, and maintaining public trust in the digital world.

In short, cybersecurity is about shielding our way of life in the increasingly interconnected digital age.

No pressure at all if you are a cybersecurity professional!

Why Choose a Career in Cybersecurity

If you are thinking about starting a career in Cybersecurity, it can seem like a complex maze of tools and terms that seem impossible to figure out. Yet, it's precisely this air of mystery and challenge that makes cybersecurity a compelling career choice.

Let's dive into the reasons why you should start a career in Cybersecurity:

- **It's a Red-Hot Market**: Cybersecurity jobs are in high demand. Despite the tech layoffs of recent times, the need for cybersecurity professionals to protect systems and data from threats continues to skyrocket. Most Job Market surveys show that the demand for Cyber Security Analysts far exceeds the supply.

- **It is Challenging:** If you enjoy solving complex problems, then a career in cybersecurity will be for you. Each day brings fresh problems, new skills to learn, and unique solutions to discover.

- **It is gratifying**: Cybersecurity professionals play a crucial role in every sector of the economy, from national security and healthcare to finance. When you thwart a phishing attack, you're not just securing data— you could be protecting a person's life savings or a company's reputation. You could prevent a breach that could shut down critical infrastructure or leak sensitive national security information. It's a field where you can make a tangible difference in the world and people's lives.

- **The Salaries are Good:** Let's face it. We do a job not out of the goodness of our hearts but because we need a weekly or monthly salary. The average pay for cybersecurity jobs is notably higher than the average for other occupations. While your starting salary can vary depending on your education, certification, and region, it tends to grow significantly as you gain experience and specialize in different areas of cybersecurity.

- **Opportunities for Growth**: The cybersecurity field is wide and varied. You might start as a Security Analyst, but you could progress to become a Security Engineer, a Penetration Tester, a Security Auditor, or even a Chief Information Security Officer (CISO). There's no set path, and the possibilities for growth are immense.
- **Continuous Learning**: With technology evolving at a breakneck pace, you'll never be at a point where you know it all. You'll always learn, evolve, and adapt to new technologies, threats, and methodologies. If lifelong learning gives you a thrill, welcome aboard the cybersecurity express!

Moreover, cybersecurity carries a certain prestige and intrigue, adding to its appeal as a career choice. While your daily job might not involve racing against the clock to stop a rogue AI from taking over the world's nuclear weapons (although, hey, you never know), there's no denying that there's something inherently awesome about working in a field that's all about outsmarting hackers, discovering vulnerabilities, and defending against cyber threats.

Finally, consider this: In a world that's increasingly connected, where data is more valuable than oil and cyber threats are a matter of when, not if, cybersecurity is no longer a niche field—it's a critical, integral part of every sector. By choosing a career in cybersecurity, you're choosing to be at the forefront of this critical battlefield, armed with knowledge, and ready to make a difference.

Debunking some myths

Now, let's debunk two popular cybersecurity myths.

- First off, cybercriminals are not usually socially awkward loners sitting in their basements. Instead, they come in all shapes and sizes, from all walks of life.
- Secondly, cybersecurity is only about preventing attacks. In reality, it's also about managing risks, ensuring compliance, creating secure networks and educating users.

Cybersecurity is a serious field with high stakes. It's about more than just catching the bad guys—it's about protecting our way of life in the digital age. I hope that makes you excited for the journey ahead.

Now, let's dive in!

2 – A Quick Overview of Cybersecurity Certifications

Armed with a solid understanding of Cybersecurity, it is time to jump into the world of Certifications. These certifications or "certs" are more than just acronyms on a resume—they are the industry's way of validating and recognizing your skills and knowledge.

There are a vast amount of certification choices or certification paths that a person can take. Each certification brings its strengths to the table and provides its unique validation.

Many accredited organizations offer these credentials, each specializing in different areas of cybersecurity. Some focus on network security, ethical hacking, information security management, and so on. Just as a Swiss army knife offers various tools for different needs, cybersecurity certifications caters to diverse interests and expertise levels within the field.

Whether you're just starting your cybersecurity journey or are an experienced professional seeking to validate and enhance your knowledge, a certification is tailored for you.

From foundational certifications like **CompTIA's Security+** for beginners to advanced ones like the **Certified Information Systems Security Professional (CISSP)** for seasoned professionals; these certifications act as milestones in your cybersecurity career, charting your growth and expertise in the field.

The Importance of Cyber Security Certifications

Imagine you are going to run a marathon. You cannot only show up on race day with preparation. You must train, understand the route, build your stamina, and perhaps even participate in shorter races to get a feel for the competition. Similarly, breaking into cybersecurity or advancing your career requires preparation and proof of your capabilities.

This is where cybersecurity certifications come into play.

Cybersecurity certifications are a badge of honour in the digital world. They validate your knowledge, skills, and commitment to the field. Certifications provide the necessary knowledge and skills and show prospective employers you're qualified for the job.

In the crowded cybersecurity job market, these certifications help you stand out. They're clear evidence to employers that you have a specific set of skills and have tried to validate these skills through a recognized certification.

With a certification, you're no longer just a candidate—you're a *certified professional,* which can give you a substantial advantage in job opportunities.

Cybersecurity certifications are also closely tied to earning potential. Various industry reports show that professionals with cybersecurity certifications tend to earn higher salaries than their non-certified counterparts. This is likely because employers are more comfortable hiring certified professionals who have demonstrated their skillset and commitment to continuing education in this demanding field.

In addition to the career and financial benefits, there's another critical reason why these certifications are essential—the learning process. Preparing for certification is an educational journey that can significantly expand your knowledge and skills. It's a focused learning path that ensures you cover all the critical aspects of a specific area in cybersecurity.

Furthermore, the importance of certifications extends beyond just when you're actively job hunting. Many cybersecurity certifications require you to recertify after a certain period or earn **Continuing Professional Education (CPE) credits**. This requirement ensures that you stay updated in your field and continue to learn and grow even after you've obtained your certification.

How to Choose the Right Certification

Choosing the proper cybersecurity certification is all about finding the right fit for your career, interests, and future goals. No matter how appealing a certificate may seem, it will only serve its purpose effectively if it aligns with your objectives and the direction you want your career to take.

To navigate this critical decision, assess your current standing and what you envision for your future. Consider the following:

- **Your current skill level**: Are you a beginner looking to gain a solid foundation or a professional seeking to deepen your specialization or broaden your overview of the field?

- **Areas of interest**: Cybersecurity is a broad field with numerous subdomains like network security, ethical hacking, security management, etc. What topics excite you the most?
- **Career goals**: Are you seeking a specific role, like a security analyst or CISO? Or you want to be a consultant or even branch into cybersecurity law.
- **Skills you wish to acquire or enhance**: Each certification emphasizes specific skills. Identify the skills you want to hone and select the certificate that best enhances them.

Research various certifications, examine their prerequisites, the skills they focus on, and the opportunities they offer, and make an informed choice. Consult professionals who have pursued these certifications, read reviews, and understand the certification's standing in the industry. After all, this is a decision that can shape your career trajectory, so make it count!

Cybersecurity Certification Levels: Beginner, Advanced, and Specialized

Cybersecurity certifications come in various types, from beginner, advanced, and specialized certifications to cater to every type of learning path.

Beginner Certifications: Perfect for those setting sail on their cybersecurity voyage. You could be a recent graduate, someone shifting career paths, or an IT professional wanting to dip your toes into cybersecurity. These certifications provide a broad overview of the field, introducing various concepts and setting a solid foundation. Think of these as your cybersecurity ABCs.

For example, CompTIA Security+ is an excellent place to start. It covers many topics, including network security and threat management, identity and access management, cryptography, etc.

Advanced Certifications: These certifications dive deeper into the field, perfect for professionals with a few years of experience wanting to validate and enhance their knowledge.

The Certified Information Systems Security Professional (CISSP) is a renowned certification at this level. This cert demonstrates a professional's expertise in designing, implementing, and managing a best-in-class cybersecurity program.

Specialized Certifications: These certifications delve into the nitty-gritty of specialized areas in cybersecurity, whether it be ethical hacking, security auditing, or cloud security.

Take, for instance, the Certified Ethical Hacker (CEH) certification. It's designed for professionals wanting to understand hackers' mindsets, tools, and tactics to better defend against them. Or consider the Certified Cloud Security Professional (CCSP) certification, ideal for those specializing in cloud security.

From the cybersecurity newbie to the specialized expert, there's a certification to mark each milestone in your career journey, enhancing your knowledge, validating your skills, and preparing you for the next exciting challenge in the dynamic field of cybersecurity.

Common Myths Around Cybersecurity Certifications

While certifications are valuable, they're often surrounded by misconceptions that can confuse and demotivate individuals. Let's debunk some of them.

Myth 1: "You need to be a techie to get into cybersecurity."

Cybersecurity is indeed a tech-heavy field, but also diverse and multidisciplinary. Many roles don't require hardcore coding skills or technical expertise. For example, cybersecurity policy analysts, legal consultants, and cybersecurity awareness trainers often need a solid understanding of the landscape without deep-diving into code. Certifications like CompTIA Security+ can cater to these less technical roles.

Myth 2: "Getting certified is enough to land a job."

While certifications can significantly boost your credibility and marketability, they're not a silver bullet. Cybersecurity employers often look for hands-on experience, problem-solving skills, communication abilities, and a keen sense of curiosity and ethical responsibility. Certification can open doors, but landing the job requires broader competencies.

Myth 3: "Cybersecurity certifications are just for cybersecurity jobs."

This can't be further from the truth. As digital transformation pervades all sectors, understanding cybersecurity has become crucial for many roles outside the field. IT professionals, project managers, network administrators, or even lawyers dealing with data privacy issues can benefit from cybersecurity certifications. They offer a solid understanding of the cybersecurity landscape, which is increasingly intertwined with almost all business functions today.

Myth 4: "Certifications are too expensive."

Some certifications indeed come with a hefty price tag, but viewing them as an investment in your career is essential. Plus, various scholarships, grants, and even employer-sponsored programs are available to cover certification costs. Additionally, not all certifications are costly. Some, like CompTIA Security+, are relatively affordable.

Myth 5: "All cybersecurity certifications are the same."

This is like saying all cars are the same because they take you from point A to point B. Each certification has a different focus, caters to a different skill level, and holds a different market value. A Certified Ethical Hacker (CEH) certification will hold a different weight or relevance than a Certified Information Security Manager (CISM) if you're pursuing a managerial role.

Conclusion

The Cybersecurity certification landscape can seem daunting when you are first starting, yet it is an essential journey for any cybersecurity professional. Choosing the right certification involves thorough research and introspection of career goals, skills, and interests. It's like fitting the right piece into your career puzzle—a correct fit can complete the picture and set you on a clear path.

In the coming chapters, we will explore the different certification paths available to help you in this journey and determine which cert works for you.

3 – The Beginner's Path

In our journey into the world of cybersecurity certifications, the first step is to understand the foundational ones that will pave the way for your career. Each of these certifications has its unique strengths, and in this chapter, we will delve into them one by one.

CompTIA Security+

CompTIA Security+ is possibly the most popular beginner-level cert in the industry. It is specifically designed to establish core cybersecurity knowledge and covers various topics like threat management, cryptography, identity management, network security, and risk identification. If you are new to cybersecurity and unsure of where to start, then this is possibly the best cert for you.

Cost and Duration: This certification is relatively budget-friendly compared to others in the field. As of 2023, the cost of the exam voucher is usually around $392, but this can vary based on your location, and the study materials can also vary in price. Depending on your study schedule, it typically takes about two to three months to prepare for the exam. However, if you're short on time or budget, numerous free or low-cost online resources are available to supplement your studies.

Career Opportunities: CompTIA Security+ is widely recognized in the job market, making it an excellent entry point into a cybersecurity career. It's typically a stepping stone to roles such as security administrators, security specialists, or network administrators.

Summary: If you're starting your journey into cybersecurity and want a broad overview of the field recognized by employers and won't break the bank, CompTIA Security+ might be your ideal companion. It's a friendly guide that helps you navigate through the fascinating world of cybersecurity. This certification is not just about expanding your knowledge— it's about opening doors to various possibilities in your cybersecurity career.

(ISC)² Certified in Cybersecurity

(ISC)² Certified in Cybersecurity is a foundational certification designed to provide a pathway into the cybersecurity industry.

It's specifically designed to validate the foundational knowledge, skills, and abilities required for an entry- or junior-level cybersecurity role. This certification is ideal for IT professionals, career changers, college students, and recent graduates.

Cost and Duration: Unlike other (ISC)² certifications, there is no work experience requirement to earn this entry-level certification. As part of their One Million Certified in Cybersecurity program, they are offering free Certified in Cybersecurity (CC) Online Self-Paced Training and exams to the first million people entering the field for the first time. . The self-paced online course, which is a recorded review session led by an authorized (ISC)² instructor, is accessible for 180 days. The duration of the exam is two hours, and it contains 100 multiple-choice test items.

Career Opportunities: The (ISC)² Certified in Cybersecurity certification is a stepping stone to roles such as security administrators, security specialists, or network administrators. It's recognized by employers as a testament to the holder's foundational knowledge in cybersecurity and their commitment to continuous learning and development in the field.

Summary: Similar to the CompTIA Securty+, if you want a certification that validates your foundational knowledge and skills, the (ISC)² Certified in Cybersecurity might be your ideal choice. It's a certification that not only expands your knowledge but also opens doors to various possibilities in your cybersecurity career. This certification is unique in that it recognizes the growing trend of people entering the cybersecurity workforce without direct IT experience, providing them with a solid grasp of the right technical concepts and a demonstrated aptitude to learn on the job.

GIAC Security Essentials (GSEC)

Next, let's consider the GIAC Security Essentials (GSEC), a certification that aims to validate the certified professional's knowledge in key areas of information security. Although still relatively introductory, the GSEC delves more in-depth and is more rigorous than Comptia Security+, delving into more advanced concepts and skills. It expects some prior knowledge or experience in IT or cybersecurity.

The GSEC coursework takes a deep dive into the technical aspects of cybersecurity, tackling areas like network protocols, password management, cryptography, and wireless security

Cost and Duration: You may find the cost of the GSEC exam relatively high as the price often exceeds $1,000. The preparation period typically ranges from 50 to 70 hours, but it can extend over a few months based on your study plan.

Career Opportunities: Earning the GSEC certification opens doors to more technical roles within the cybersecurity field. These could include positions such as information security analyst, network security engineer, or IT auditor.

Summary: If you're ready for a more technical deep dive into cybersecurity and willing to invest time and money into your education, the GIAC Security Essentials (GSEC) certification might be your perfect fit. It's the challenging and rewarding trail that takes you through the dense forests of cybersecurity while teaching you invaluable survival skills. So pack your bags, lace up your boots, and prepare for an unforgettable cybersecurity adventure!

(ISC)² Systems Security Certified Practitioner (SSCP)

Moving on, the (ISC)² Systems Security Certified Practitioner (SSCP) serves as a valuable certification for IT administrators, managers, directors, and network security professionals. The SSCP covers seven domains of IT security, including access controls, administration, risk identification, incident response and recovery, cryptography, networks and communications, and systems and application security.

Cost and Duration: The cost for the SSCP exam typically falls around $250, making it a relatively affordable investment for the wealth of knowledge it offers. Depending on your commitment and existing knowledge, preparing for the SSCP exam could take from a few weeks to a few months.

Career Opportunities: Earning the SSCP certification can lead to various positions in the IT security field, such as network security engineer, security analyst, and systems/network administrator.

Summary: If you're a seasoned IT professional looking to delve into the specifics of system security or a newbie wanting to learn the ropes from a system's security perspective, the (ISC)² Systems Security Certified Practitioner (SSCP) could be the perfect certification for you. It offers you a comprehensive guide to the scenic routes and major highways of systems security, ultimately helping you become a skilled driver in the cybersecurity world. Buckle up, and enjoy the ride!

Certified of Cloud Security Knowledge (CCSK)

More and more companies are moving critical workloads towards providers like Microsoft Azure, Amazon Web Services (AWS), Google Cloud, etc. and cloud-specific security skills are red-hot in demand. Recognizing this necessity, the Cloud Security Alliance (CSA) developed the Certificate of Cloud Security Knowledge (CCSK), one of the leading certifications focusing exclusively on cloud security. It is designed to ensure professionals comprehensively understand cloud security challenges and best practices. The CCSK is a widely recognized certification validates an individual's competence in key cloud security areas. If you are interested in diving directly into the cloud and getting foundational knowledge, then this is the cert for you

It covers a broad spectrum of cloud security concepts based on the CSA's "Security Guidance for Critical Areas of Focus in Cloud Computing V4.0" and the ENISA's "Cloud Computing Risk Assessment." The coursework includes cloud computing concepts and architectures, governance and risk management, legal issues, compliance and audit management, information management and data security, securing cloud infrastructure, and application security.

Cost and Duration: At USD 395, the CCSK examination fee is relatively affordable, with training courses and materials available at additional costs. The preparation time can vary depending on one's familiarity with the concepts, typically ranging from a few weeks to a few months.

Career Opportunities: Earning the CCSK certification enhances your career opportunities in various cloud-related roles, such as cloud security specialist, cloud architect, security administrator, system administrator, and more. It's an ideal credential for professionals engaged in managing or securing cloud environments and for consultants guiding organizations through cloud transitions. It's also useful for risk and compliance professionals who require an understanding of cloud-specific risks.

Summary: The CCSK is a highly respected and globally recognized certification for professionals seeking to demonstrate a strong understanding of cloud security principles. Its comprehensive coverage of key cloud security areas and vendor-neutral stance make it a valuable certification for individuals dealing with cloud environments.

Google Cybersecurity Professional Certificate: The New Kid on the Block

Google, the tech behemoth we all know and love, is now expanding its horizons into cybersecurity education. The launch of the Google Cybersecurity Professional Certificate is introducing a fresh, user-friendly, and accessible entry point into the cybersecurity field. The Google Cybersecurity Professional Certificate is a program designed for absolute beginners—no prior experience is needed. The program structure starts with a foundational module and progresses to technical topics like SQL, Linux, and Python, culminating with a module on preparing for Cybersecurity jobs.

The certificate consists of eight modules, each exploring a distinct aspect of cybersecurity. The courses range from "Foundations of Cybersecurity" and "Connect and Protect: Networks and Network Security" to more advanced courses like "Automate Cybersecurity Tasks with Python." It's a blend of general overviews and technical skill building, giving you a well-rounded foundation in cybersecurity.

Cost and Duration: Coursera, the hosting platform, charges $49 a month for this certificate program. Google estimates that you can complete it in about six months by dedicating around seven hours a week. If you're more ambitious and can commit to 7-10 hours a week, you could complete it in three months.

However, if you're on a tight budget, you can audit the courses for free, although this won't include a certificate.

Career Opportunities: Google is known for its name in the industry and the high quality programs they provide; this program is no exception. As part of their "Grow with Google" initiative, they regularly partner with businesses and universities to connect graduates with job opportunities. This is definitely a cert to keep an eye on as Google puts more of its massive backing behind it.

Choosing the Right Certification

Choosing the right certification is a crucial step in your cybersecurity journey. It's not just about the cost or the popularity—it's about finding the certification that aligns with your career goals, matches your skill level, and fits your budget. So, take your time, do your research, and embark on the journey that will transform your career.

You can use the below table as a useful reference point.

Certification	Cost	Preparation Time	Career Opportunities	Best For

Certification	Cost	Preparation Time	Career Opportunities	Best For
CompTIA Security+	~$392	2-3 months	Security Administrators, Security Specialists, Network Administrators	Beginners, budget-conscious individuals, and those wanting a broad foundation
GIAC Security Essentials (GSEC)	>$1,000	50-70 hours (possibly extending over months)	Information Security Analyst, Network Security Engineer, IT Auditor	Those ready for a deeper dive into cybersecurity and have a higher budget
(ISC)² Certified in Cybersecurity	Currently free	Self-paced online course accessible for 180	Entry- or junior-level roles in cybersecurity, such as security administrators,	IT professionals, career changers, college

Certification	Cost	Preparati on Time	Career Opportunities	Best For
		days. Exam duration is two hours.	security specialists, or network administrators.	students, and recent graduates looking to enter the cybersecurity field.
(ISC)² Systems Security Certified Practitioner (SSCP)	~$250	Few weeks to few months	Network Security Engineer, Security Analyst, Systems/Network Administrator	IT professionals and those interested in system security specifics
Certificate of Cloud Security Knowledge (CCSK)	~$395	Varies (a few weeks to a few months)	Cloud Security Specialist, Cloud Architect, Security Administrator, System Administrator	Professionals dealing with or transitioning to cloud environments

Certification	Cost	Preparation Time	Career Opportunities	Best For
Google Cybersecurity Professional Certificate	$49/month (complete in ~6 months)	~6 months (7 hours/week)	Various, as Google connects graduates with opportunities	Absolute beginners and those interested in job opportunities through Google's network

Summary

In conclusion, cybersecurity offers a diverse array of certifications tailored for beginners. Each one offers unique benefits and caters to different interests, budgets, and career goals. The CompTIA Security+ and Google Cybersecurity Professional Certificate provide a broad foundational knowledge at a relatively low cost, making them ideal starting points for those new to the field. For those ready to invest more, the GSEC and SSCP delve into technical knowledge, while the CCSK zeroes in on the increasingly important area of cloud security. Each of these certifications paves the way to a variety of career opportunities in the cybersecurity field. Remember, the best certification for you aligns with your career aspirations, available resources, and specific areas of interest within the vast landscape of cybersecurity.

4 – The Intermediate to Advanced Path

Now that we have a solid understanding of the foundational level certifications let us move towards the intermediate to advanced levels. These certifications focus on more advanced areas and are suited for those individuals who have several years of experience under their belt. Let us look at a few of the most popular advanced-level certifications within the industry.

Certified Information Systems Security Professional (CISSP)

Industry experts consider the CISSP the "gold standard" of cybersecurity certifications for good reason. It is an advanced-level certification for IT security professionals that has been popular for decades.

Coursework: The CISSP covers eight domains of IT security, including Security and Risk Management, Asset Security, Security Architecture and Engineering, Communication, Network Security, Identity and Access Management (IAM), Security Assessment and Testing, Security Operations, and Software Development Security. It's like a comprehensive map detailing every key location in cybersecurity.

Cost and Duration: The CISSP exam costs about $699, which can be a substantial investment. Preparing for the CISSP exam, depending on your existing knowledge and dedication, could take several weeks to a few months.

Career Opportunities: With the CISSP under your belt, you could qualify for positions like IT Director, Security Analyst, and even Chief Information Security Officer (CISO). It's like reaching the summit of a mountain and having a panoramic view of your career possibilities.

Summary: If you're an IT professional looking to step into a leadership role in cybersecurity, the Certified Information Systems Security Professional (CISSP) would be a key certification goal to achieve. It's challenging and demanding, but the view (read, opportunities) is unparalleled at the top.

Certified Information Security Manager (CISM)

Like the CISSP, the Certified Information Security Manager (CISM) also targets professionals at a more senior level. It is a globally respected certification focusing on the management and governance of information security.

Coursework: The CISM covers four main domains: Information Security Governance, Information Risk Management, Information Security Program Development and Management, and Information Security Incident Management. It has a more strategic focus on Cybersecurity than the CISSP, which contains a mixture of strategic and technical domains.

Cost and Duration: The cost of the CISM exam is around $575—a significant investment again! Preparation time could range from several weeks to a few months, depending on your familiarity with the coursework.

Career Opportunities: The CISM could lead to roles such as IT Security Manager, IT Auditor, IT Consultant, and even the CISO; allowing you to command respect and a handsome paycheck.

Summary: The CISM is for those ready to step into management roles, effectively strategizing and governing information security. It's a challenging cert, but it can be achieved easily with the proper preparation and attitude.

CISSP vs. CISM (The Author's 100% subjective opinion)

A common question is whether an experienced professional should go with the CISSP or CISM when planning for a more advanced level cert. Both are easily the most popular certifications in the industry and choosing the right one largely depends on your career path.

The CISSP is best suited for IT professionals aiming to be security architects, consultants, or analysts who love the adrenaline rush of hands-on technical work. The CISSP is the peak for those who wish to demonstrate their technical and managerial competence in information security.

On the other hand, CISM has a more strategic focus. CISM is your goal if you dream of managerial roles, where your primary responsibility isn't the trenches of day-to-day technical work but governing and managing a company's security practices. The CISM's strength is its emphasis on management and strategy, ideal for future information security managers or IT consultants.

Your choice of certification should align with your personal preferences and professional aspirations.

For hands-on security professionals aiming to prove their technical chops and managerial skills in information security, the CISSP would be an ideal fit. On the other hand, for those who are looking to step into strategic roles, managing and governing information security, CISM would be their mountain to conquer.

Remember, both are challenging ascents promising rewarding views. The choice depends on what you want your cybersecurity journey to look like and the vantage point you wish to conquer.

Cybersecurity Analyst (CySA+)

The CompTIA Cybersecurity Analyst (CySA+) is the big brother of the CompTIA Security+, which we discussed in the previous chapter. The certification focuses on the skills needed for threat management, vulnerability management, and cyber incident response. It is ideal for professionals who want to become trusted subject matter experts within Cybersecurity.

Coursework: The CySA+ covers vital topics like threat and vulnerability management, software and systems security, security operations and monitoring, and incident response.

Cost and Duration: The cost of the CySA+ exam is around $392 which can increase if you add in their training bundles also. The preparation time can range from weeks to months, depending on your pre-existing knowledge and study dedication. It's a journey worth taking, requiring patience and preparation.

Career Opportunities: Earning the CySA+ can open doors to roles such as Threat Intelligence Analyst, Security Analyst, Application Security Analyst, and Compliance Analyst.

Summary: The CompTIA Cybersecurity Analyst (CySA+) certification is an excellent choice for those who wish to specialize in analyzing, managing, and mitigating threats, turning the uncertain terrain of cybersecurity into a navigable landscape.

Certified Cloud Security Professional (CCSP)

Think of the Certified Cloud Security Professional (CCSP) as a distant cousin to the CISSP, but with a focus on Cloud Security. It is a globally recognized certification that showcases your knowledge and skills in cloud security architecture, design, operations, and service orchestration.

Coursework: The CCSP covers six domains: Cloud Concepts, Architecture and Design, Cloud Data Security, Cloud Platform & Infrastructure Security, Cloud Application Security, Cloud Security Operations, and Legal, Risk, and Compliance.

Cost and Duration: The cost of the CCSP exam is about $599—not cheap by any means! Preparation time typically ranges from a few weeks to several months, depending on your previous experience and study plan.

Career Opportunities: The CCSP can lead to roles such as Cloud Security Architect, Cloud Security Engineer, Security Administrator, Systems Engineer, and more. With the CCSP, you're not just an explorer on the ground but a pioneer in the cloud, leading the way in this new frontier.

Summary: The Certified Cloud Security Professional (CCSP) is an ideal certification for those ready to soar into the world of cloud security, leading the way in securing this vast, evolving landscape.

Choosing the Right Certification

Now comes the big question—how do you choose? It's simple—your choice should align with your career goals, financial capability, existing skill level, and the cybersecurity domain you're interested in. If you're an experienced professional aiming for leadership roles, CISSP or CISM could be the right fit. Or are you someone intrigued by the vast cloud security industry? Then CCSP might be your calling.

Use the below table as a general guide, and visit the individual certification websites for the most current information and requirements.

Please note that the "Cost" column signifies the cost of the exam and not the total cost of preparation which can vary based on study materials and courses.

Certification	Cost	Career Opportunities	Summary
Certified Information Systems Security Professional (CISSP)	$699	IT Director, Security Analyst, Chief Information Security Officer (CISO)	Ideal for IT professionals aiming to demonstrate their technical and managerial competence in information security and looking for leadership roles in cybersecurity
Certified Information Security Manager (CISM)	$575	IT Security Manager, IT Auditor, IT Consultant, CISO	Best suited for professionals ready to step into management roles, strategizing and governing information security effectively
Cybersecurity Analyst (CySA+)	$392	Threat Intelligence Analyst, Security Analyst, Application Security Analyst, Compliance Analyst	Excellent for those who wish to specialize in analyzing, managing, and mitigating threats

Certification	Cost	Career Opportunities	Summary
Certified Cloud Security Professional (CCSP)	$599	Cloud Security Architect, Cloud Security Engineer, Security Administrator, Systems Engineer	Ideal for professionals ready to focus on cloud security, providing a solid foundation in securing the evolving cloud landscape

Summary

In conclusion, advancing your career in cybersecurity requires a comprehensive understanding of both foundational and higher-level certifications. As we've seen, each certification has unique domains, costs, preparation times, and career opportunities. They serve different career paths and roles within the industry, from technical to managerial and strategic positions. The choice between these certifications will largely depend on your career goals and areas of interest. Whether you're just starting your cybersecurity journey or looking to scale new heights, a certification will help you navigate your path and reach your professional summit.

5 – Specialized Certification Pathways

Now that we have covered the foundational and advanced aspects of Cybersecurity Certifications let us look at the specialized path. Some professionals do not want a high-level understanding and instead want to become subject matter experts in a particular area. This is where the specialized path comes in.

As a Cybersecurity specialist, you must hone specific skills to thrive in your area. A network security expert needs a different toolkit than a cloud security engineer, and a penetration tester needs to think differently than an incident response handler. Let us take a look at these areas in detail!

Penetration Testing

Certified Ethical Hacker (CEH)

Beginners stepping into the mysterious world of penetration testing often aim for the Certified Ethical Hacker (CEH) certification. Its aim is to give you the knowledge you need to start your career in ethical hacking and penetration testing.

Coursework: The CEH curriculum consists of 20 comprehensive modules. These range from exploring the crevices of system hacking to the labyrinth of SQL injection, from the curious world of virus analysis to the burgeoning domain of IoT hacking. With over 340 attack technologies, CEH offers a rich, practical environment to understand and anticipate the hacker's perspective.

Cost and Duration: The investment you need for the CEH exam stands around $1,199. You should allocate about six weeks of part-time study to traverse this extensive course comfortably.

Career Opportunities: Once armed with the CEH certification, you're primed for roles like penetration tester, vulnerability assessor, or security analyst. The demand for ethical hackers has been consistently high, and with the increasing digital threats, it's only set to rise. Organizations across various sectors are recognizing the value of proactive cybersecurity, increasing the demand for professionals with a CEH certification.

Summary: The CEH certification is a robust introduction to the world of ethical hacking, offering a comprehensive perspective on various hacking techniques and tools. It acts as a launchpad for those beginning their journey in cybersecurity or those with a couple of years in IT security, preparing to venture into more specialized roles. With an exam fee of $1,199, the CEH is a significant investment. However, the comprehensive curriculum and industry recognition it brings can offer a significant return on investment, especially for those new to the field.

Offensive Security Certified Professional (OSCP)

The Offensive Security Certified Professional (OSCP) is one of the most respected certs within penetration testing. It validates your practical knowledge and proves you can think on your feet in real-world network security scenarios. The OSCP is known for its rigorous hands-on exam, where you must successfully exploit several machines in 24 hours. It requires a deep understanding of various exploitation techniques and a lot of practice. As such, it is generally considered more challenging than most other certifications.

What is it and Coursework: The OSCP journey begins with the course 'Penetration Testing with Kali Linux (PWK),' which spans modules such as password cracking, privilege escalation, and client-side attacks. The unique aspect of this certification is its hands-on approach, where you must compromise a virtual network's security in a 24-hour exam to claim the OSCP title.

Cost and Duration: The course fee, including 30-day lab access and the exam fee, is around $1599. If you want to thoroughly cover the course material and practice in the labs, you should allow yourself about 2-3 months. The OSCP certification costs around $1599, including the course and exam fee. While this may seem high, it is comparable to other professional certifications in the field, and the hands-on experience gained is often considered invaluable.

Career Opportunities: Penetration testers are in high demand across many sectors. The OSCP, in particular, is well-regarded and often considered a prerequisite for many advanced cybersecurity roles. Earning an OSCP puts you in a favourable position for roles such as penetration tester, security engineer, and cybersecurity consultant.

Summary: The OSCP certification is a testament to a person's practical expertise in penetration testing. Its rigorous, hands-on approach equips you with real-world problem-solving skills, distinguishing you in the job market. The OSCP certification is highly recommended for anyone specializing in penetration testing. It offers real-world skills that are highly valued in the cybersecurity market, making it an excellent choice for those looking to elevate their career to the next level.

Certified Ethical Hacker (CEH) vs. Offensive Security Certified Professional (OSCP)

Deciding between the CEH and the OSCP can be a difficult choice. While both are geared towards ethical hacking and penetration testing, they each offer a unique approach and cater to different skill levels. Below is a comparison table to help you make the best decision for your career path.

Criteria	Certified Ethical Hacker (CEH)	Offensive Security Certified Professional (OSCP)
Purpose	To validate the knowledge of network security professionals in ethical hacking.	To validate the practical skills of IT security professionals in penetration testing.

Criteria	Certified Ethical Hacker (CEH)	Offensive Security Certified Professional (OSCP)
Approach	Mostly theoretical, focusing on the understanding of potential vulnerabilities and tools.	Mostly practical, focusing on real-world attack simulations and problem-solving skills.
Exam Format	Multiple choice questions.	24-hour practical exam where you must compromise a virtual network's security.
Difficulty Level	Beginner to intermediate level.	Intermediate to advanced level, often considered a challenging certification.
Cost	Around $1,199 (Includes training and exam voucher).	Around $1599 (Including course and exam fees).
Market Recognition	Globally recognized and widely accepted.	Highly respected among employers who need hands-on penetration testers.
Pre-requisites	No formal prerequisites, but knowledge of networking and IT security is beneficial.	Basic knowledge of Linux and networking, along with some experience in information security.

In conclusion, if you're just beginning your journey into penetration testing, the CEH could be a great starting point. It provides a broad understanding of the various tools and techniques used in ethical hacking. On the other hand, if you're seeking a hands-on certification that can provide practical experience and challenge your problem-solving skills, the OSCP would be a suitable choice. Ultimately, your choice should align with your career goals, existing skills, and learning preferences.

Cloud Security

In previous chapters, we discussed the CCSK and CCSP cloud security certifications, which are both technology-agnostic certifications, i.e., the concepts in those exams can be applied to any cloud environment. As more and more organizations move their operations to the cloud, the demand for specialized cloud security professionals is on the rise. These certifications validate your knowledge and skills in securing particular cloud environments. This section covers three prominent cloud security certifications - Azure Security Engineer, AWS Security, and Google Cloud Security Engineer.

Azure Security Engineer

Microsoft's Azure Security Engineer Associate certification (AZ-500) gives you the skills to implement security controls, manage identity and access, and protect data, applications, and networks in in the Microsoft Azure Cloud environment.

What is it?

This certification forms part of the more extensive journey toward developing end-to-end infrastructure solutions. It's a testament to your expertise in managing security operations and securing data and applications on Azure, Microsoft's popular cloud platform.

Coursework and Content

The certification covers a wide range of topics, including identity and access management, implementation of platform protection, managing security operations, and securing data and applications on Azure.

Cost and Duration

The cost of the exam is approximately $165. The duration largely depends on your knowledge and experience with Azure and security concepts. With consistent study, it may take a few months to prepare for the exam adequately.

Career Opportunities

As a certified Azure Security Engineer, you'll find numerous opportunities in the ever-growing cloud market. Many organizations, especially those already using Azure, seek certified professionals to help them safeguard their cloud operations.

Summary

The Azure Security Engineer Associate certification is a worthy consideration for any IT professional looking to delve into the cloud security domain. The certification cost is reasonable, given its potential return on investment. However, it's important to note that the complexity of the certification could pose a challenge for beginners. Nevertheless, with the continuous growth of Azure, market demand for Azure Security Engineers remains robust. If you're aiming for a career that merges the worlds of cloud and security, this certification could be a strong contender.

AWS Security Specialty

With the AWS Certified Security - Specialty certification from Amazon Web Services (AWS), you can demonstrate your ability to effectively secure the AWS platform. It validates your understanding of intricate data classifications, data encryption methods, and secure internet protocols

What is it?

This specialty-level certification focuses on your skill set to secure AWS workloads and use security controls for workloads on AWS.

Coursework and Content

The AWS Certified Security - Specialty certification is quite comprehensive. It covers incident response, logging and monitoring, infrastructure security, identity and access management, and data protection.

Cost and Duration

The cost to sit for the exam is approximately $300. The preparation duration is subjective and hinges largely on your familiarity with AWS security practices and principles.

Typically, for individuals with some experience, a few months of diligent study should suffice.

Career Opportunities

With AWS being a global leader in cloud computing, AWS security professionals are sought after by organizations worldwide. An AWS Certified Security - Specialty credential can open the door to roles such as AWS Security Specialist, Security Analyst, Security Architect, and more.

Summary

The AWS Certified Security - Specialty certification is a valuable choice if you're keen to focus on the security aspects of AWS. Although the certification costs a bit higher than others, the potential return for career advancement makes it a worthwhile investment. In terms of difficulty, it does require a solid understanding of AWS and its security measures, meaning that beginners may find it challenging. However, with AWS's undisputed market dominance, the demand for AWS Certified Security - Specialty professionals remains high. It's an excellent option for those looking to specialize in the security aspect of AWS.

Google Professional Cloud Security Engineer

Google's Professional Cloud Security Engineer certification signifies your ability to design and implement a secure infrastructure on the Google Cloud Platform (GCP). This certificate proves your ability to configure network security defenses and ensure data integrity and access controls.

What is it?

This professional-level certification from Google Cloud requires knowledge of the Google Cloud product suite and the industry's best practices for cloud security.

Coursework and Content

The certification content spans a range of topics, including configuring access within a cloud solution environment, ensuring data protection, configuring network security defenses, analyzing and managing threats, and managing operational, regulatory, and compliance concerns.

Cost and Duration

The exam costs about $200. The duration to prepare for this certification will primarily depend on your prior experience with Google Cloud and security principles. On average, a couple of months of dedicated study might be enough for professionals already familiar with the basics.

Career Opportunities

With this certification, you can be recognized as a Google Professional Cloud Security Engineer, opening doors to roles such as Cloud Security Specialist, GCP Security Analyst, and more. Businesses increasingly adopting GCP means growing opportunities for GCP-certified professionals.

Summary

The Google Professional Cloud Security Engineer certification is a notable choice for those interested in pursuing a career in cloud security, specifically within the GCP environment. Though the cost of the certificate is on par with others in this field, it's essential to consider the slight learning curve, especially for those new to Google Cloud. But considering the rising popularity and demand for Google Cloud services in the market, this certification could significantly boost your career in cloud security.

Network Security

Network security is a critical aspect of information technology that aims to protect an organization's network infrastructure from various threats, including unauthorized access, data breaches, and cyber-attacks. It involves implementing multiple layers of defenses within and at the network's edge. Every layer has controls and policies designed to combat threats and prevent unauthorized access to data.

CCNP Security

The Cisco Certified Network Professional (CCNP) Security certification attests to your ability to manage security in a networking environment. Specifically, it demonstrates your expertise in securing Cisco's network devices.

What is it?

This is a professional-level certification offered by Cisco, one of the leaders in networking technology. It validates your advanced technical skills and knowledge in network security.

Coursework and Content

The CCNP Security certification covers various topics, including securing access to network devices, understanding and implementing end-to-end secure network designs, and managing a robust security infrastructure.

Cost and Duration

The cost to sit for the certification exams is approximately $1200, split across multiple modules. The preparation duration can vary depending on your experience level, but a few months of diligent study is typically recommended.

Career Opportunities

With a CCNP Security certification, you can land roles such as a Network Security Engineer, Network Security Specialist, or Security Administrator. Cisco's broad usage in organizations worldwide ensures a steady demand for skilled professionals.

Summary

The CCNP Security certification is an excellent choice for those seeking to specialize in network security, specifically in a Cisco environment. While the certification cost may be a bit higher than others, the depth of knowledge and skills it offers could be a significant booster for your career. In terms of difficulty, it does demand a solid understanding of network security, so beginners might find it challenging. Nonetheless, given Cisco's significant market presence, the demand for CCNP Security certified professionals is undeniably high. It's a solid certification for those looking to advance in network security.

Incident Response

Incident response is an organized approach to addressing and managing the aftermath of a security breach or cyberattack, also known as an incident. The objective is to manage the situation to limit damage, reduce recovery time and costs, and mitigate negative impacts on an organization. In the era of increasing cyber threats, responding effectively to incidents is a critical skill in cybersecurity.

GIAC Certified Incident Handler (GCIH)

The Global Information Assurance Certification (GIAC) Certified Incident Handler (GCIH) certification affirms your ability to manage incidents; understand standard attack techniques, vectors, and tools; and defend against and respond to such attacks when they occur.

What is it?

The GCIH is a globally recognized certification in the cybersecurity field, focusing on handling and responding to various security incidents. GIAC, a trusted entity known for its practical, job-specific certifications, offers it.

Coursework and Content

The GCIH covers critical aspects of incident handling, such as detecting, responding, and resolving computer security incidents in a practical environment. The certification introduces you to standard attack techniques and processes to exploit software vulnerabilities and incident handling phases like preparation, identification, containment, eradication, and recovery.

Cost and Duration

The certification exam costs approximately $1,299 with an additional cost if taken with training. Preparation time typically ranges between a few weeks to a couple of months, depending on your familiarity with the content and the amount of time you can devote to studying each week.

Career Opportunities

A GCIH certification can lead to roles such as Incident Handler, Security Analyst, or Penetration Tester. Incident response is critical to any organization's cybersecurity strategy, so the demand for GCIH-certified professionals is growing consistently.

Summary

If you want to specialize in incident response, the GCIH is a strong choice. It may be a bit more expensive than other certifications, but it provides detailed, practical knowledge that will be directly applicable to roles in incident handling. About difficulty, it requires a good understanding of various attack techniques and incident response strategies. The demand for GCIH professionals is high due to the constant need for organizations to prepare for and respond to cybersecurity incidents.

Choosing the Right Certification

With cybersecurity's vast domain, finding the specialization that aligns with your interests, career aspirations, and strengths can be challenging. Begin by assessing your current skill set and interests. Are you more intrigued by network or cloud security, or does the thrill of hunting down cyber threats through penetration testing appeal to you? Your passion will fuel those long nights of study or challenging projects.

Next, consider the job market and future trends. Look at job postings in your desired field, consult professionals already in the field, and research predictions for future cybersecurity needs. Keep an eye out for emerging technologies like cloud or IoT, as specializations in these areas are rapidly growing in demand.

Finally, consider each certification's cost, difficulty level, and commitment. While cost should not be the deciding factor, evaluating whether the investment will yield the desired return regarding career progression, salary increase, or job opportunities is essential.

Summary

As we conclude this thrilling expedition into the expansive terrain of specialized cybersecurity certifications, one truth remains paramount: the right choice is entirely subjective, resting on the unique intersection of your interests, career goals, current skill sets, and market trends.

Remember, the cybersecurity landscape and its opportunities are vast and ever-evolving. So, whether you're a novice cyber explorer or a seasoned cybersecurity mountaineer, there's always a new peak to conquer.

6 – Common Mistakes to Avoid

Navigating the path to cybersecurity certification is akin to walking through a minefield, filled with potential pitfalls that can derail your journey. In this chapter we'll delve into common blunders committed by newcomers as they dive headfirst into their first certification.

These mistakes can rob you of your precious time, hard-earned money, and worst of all, they can lead to frustration and disappointment that can dampen even the most resilient spirits.

From choosing the wrong certification for your career goals to the pitfalls of the notorious 'Certification Factory' syndrome, we will cover these mistakes so that you know when and how to avoid them.

Choosing the Right Certification: Common Missteps

Consider the case of Alex, a budding cybersecurity professional. Alex saw that many of his peers were pursuing the Certified Ethical Hacker (CEH) certification. It was trending in the industry, and Alex, not wanting to be left behind, decided to jump on the bandwagon. However, Alex's career goal was to specialize in cybersecurity risk management, a field where the Certified Information Systems Security Professional (CISSP) certification would have been more beneficial.

Despite his best efforts, Alex struggled with the CEH material, which focused heavily on penetration testing and network security—areas that didn't align with his career goals or previous experience. He found the exam challenging and, unfortunately, did not pass on his first attempt. Even after eventually obtaining the CEH certification, Alex found that it didn't provide the career advancement he had hoped for. Employers in his desired field were more interested in candidates with risk management certifications like the CISSP. Alex's story serves as a cautionary tale about the importance of choosing the right certification that aligns with your career goals.

Starting your certification journey can be an exciting time and it is important not to rush into it. Choosing the right certification requires thought, patience, and a good understanding of what your career goals are. Let us delve into the common missteps that can happen to ensure that you can sidestep these mistakes on your cybersecurity journey.

Mistake 1 - Jumping on the Bandwagon: Often, novices and even seasoned professionals make the mistake of selecting a certification just because it's trending or because their peers are pursuing it. Called it "the shiny cert" syndrome. While it's essential to stay updated with market trends, blindly jumping on the bandwagon without understanding if the certification aligns with your career goals or skill set is a recipe for disaster.

Mistake 2 - Biting off More Than You Can Chew: Ambition is great, but overestimating your abilities can lead to wasted time, money, and demotivation. Picking a certification beyond your current skill level is akin to trying to climb Everest without prior mountaineering experience. Choose a certification that matches your current abilities and gradually work your way up.

Mistake 3 - Neglecting Market Demand: Not all certifications are created equal, and the market demand for certain certifications might be higher than others. It's crucial to understand which certifications employers value and which are in demand in the job market. Ignoring market trends can leave you with a certification that, while impressive, doesn't hold much weight in the real world.

Mistake 4 - Overestimating the Power of Certifications: A certification is not a magical key that will automatically open doors to high-paying jobs. Many novices make the mistake of thinking that a certification alone will suffice. It's important to remember that while a certification can enhance your CV, it can't replace hands-on experience, problem-solving abilities, and soft skills.

If you are thinking about how to avoid these mistakes? Here are some tips to help you:

Do your Research: Before selecting a certification, spend time researching it. Understand what skills it imparts, its relevance in the market, the prerequisites, and the examination process. Look beyond flashy titles and delve into the nitty-gritty.

Realistic Self-Assessment: Be honest with yourself about your current skills and knowledge level. It's better to start with a beginner-level certification and work your way up than to aim too high and fall short.

Seeking Mentorship: A mentor, preferably someone experienced in the field of cybersecurity, can offer invaluable advice on which certification to pursue based on your career goals and current skill set. They can also provide you with practical insights that you won't find in books or online.

Consider Long-Term Career Goals: Always align your choice of certification with your long-term career aspirations. Are you interested in cloud security, ethical hacking, or perhaps network security? Choose a certification that will propel you towards your chosen path.

How to Choose The Rigth Cert

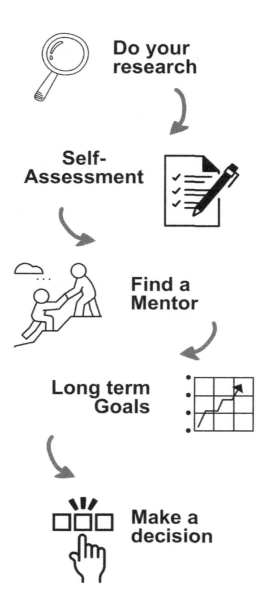

Do your research

Self-Assessment

Find a Mentor

Long term Goals

Make a decision

Choosing the right cybersecurity certification is a crucial decision that requires careful thought, research, and planning. Avoid these common missteps, and you'll be well on your way to a rewarding cybersecurity career.

Exam Preparation Blunders

Let's take the example of Sarah, an aspiring cybersecurity professional preparing for her first certification exam. Sarah had a busy schedule and kept postponing her study sessions, thinking she could cram all the material in the week before the exam. When the week before the exam arrived, Sarah found herself overwhelmed with the volume of material she needed to cover. She spent long nights trying to memorize everything, but the information just didn't stick.

On the day of the exam, Sarah quickly realized that her cramming strategy had failed. She struggled to recall key concepts and couldn't apply the theoretical knowledge to the practical scenarios presented in the exam questions. Unfortunately, Sarah did not pass the exam. This experience taught her a valuable lesson about the importance of a steady study routine. For her next attempt, Sarah started studying well in advance, scheduling regular, manageable study sessions. This approach allowed her to fully understand and retain the material, leading to a successful exam outcome.

Just like choosing the right certification requires a proper plan, preparation also requires a clear strategy to avoid these common missteps

Mistake 1 - Cramming: The arch-nemesis of effective learning, cramming, has been the downfall of many aspiring cybersecurity professionals. These certifications are not a sprint but a marathon, requiring consistent effort and understanding over time. Attempting to absorb weeks or months' worth of material in a few feverish late-night study sessions rarely ends well. It's like trying to eat an entire feast in one gulp - you'll end up with indigestion or worse!

Mistake 2 - Reliance on Theoretical Knowledge: Cybersecurity is a practical field. Solely relying on theoretical knowledge, without understanding its application, is akin to learning to swim on dry land. You might know the strokes, but will you stay afloat when tossed into the deep end? Many aspirants make the mistake of focusing only on memorizing information without understanding how to apply it in real-world scenarios.

Mistake 3 - Underestimating the Exam Structure: A common mistake is underestimating the importance of understanding the exam structure. Walking into the exam without understanding the format is like wandering into a jungle without a map or compass. You'll end up lost, confused, and panicked. Each exam has its unique format, and understanding it can give you a significant advantage.

Mistake 4 - Ignoring Practice Exams: Practice makes perfect. Yet, many hopefuls ignore the value of practice exams, viewing them as unnecessary or a waste of time. Practice exams not only help familiarize you with the exam format but also serve as an effective measure of your readiness. Ignoring them is like refusing to do a dress rehearsal before the big show.

Now that we've identified these blunders let's explore how to avoid them and ensure a smooth and successful exam preparation journey.

Building a Steady Study Routine: Consistency is key when preparing for a cybersecurity certification exam. Build a study schedule that allows for regular, manageable study sessions over a prolonged period. Block time in your calendar as that will ensure you have consistency day in and day out. This helps in better retention and understanding of the material.

Combining Theoretical Learning with Practical Application: Whenever possible, try to apply the theoretical knowledge you've learned. This could be through lab exercises, real-world projects, or even simulations. This will give you a deeper understanding of the concepts and how they are applied in real-life scenarios.

Understanding the Exam Structure: Spend time understanding the structure of the exam. Know the types of questions, the duration, the passing score, and any other important details. This will not only help you create an effective study plan but also reduce exam day anxiety.

Taking Practice Exams: Regularly take practice exams throughout your study period. They serve as excellent indicators of your preparedness and help you identify areas of weakness. Consider them as your mock battles before the actual war.

In conclusion, preparing for a cybersecurity certification exam is a strategic endeavour. Avoiding these common blunders will not only ease your preparation journey but also significantly increase your chances of passing the exam and earning the certification that could be a game-changer in your cybersecurity career.

Unrealistic Career Expectations

The ever-evolving landscape of cybersecurity, while thrilling, often carries with it a cloud of misconceptions. These misconceptions tend to form unrealistic career expectations in the minds of aspiring professionals. Let's debunk these fallacies and lay the foundation for establishing achievable career goals in this exciting domain.

Instant Success Post Certification: A common myth is that earning a cybersecurity certification equals instant success. It's crucial to remember that while certifications can provide a strong knowledge base and demonstrate commitment to the field, they are not golden tickets to immediate success. They can open doors, but climbing the ladder requires more than just a piece of paper.

Underestimating the Importance of Experience: The cybersecurity world places tremendous value on real-world experience. Many newcomers overlook this fact, believing that a certification alone is enough to land a high-level role. This misconception can lead to frustration when reality doesn't match expectations. Certifications, while beneficial, cannot replace the insights, skills, and judgment developed through practical experience.

Overlooking Continuous Learning: Cybersecurity is an incredibly dynamic field, with new threats and technologies emerging constantly. Hence, learning in this field is a continuous journey, not a one-time event. Many newbies neglect this aspect, assuming that once certified, further learning isn't necessary. This mistake can be a career-limiting move in an industry driven by constant evolution.

Having discussed these misconceptions, let's delve into strategies for cultivating realistic and achievable career expectations in cybersecurity.

Understanding Certifications as Stepping Stones: Certifications are stepping stones on the path to a successful cybersecurity career, not magical expressways. They can provide a solid foundation of knowledge, validate skills, and even give a competitive edge in job applications. However, they are not a replacement for experience, dedication, and continuous learning.

Valuing Practical Experience: A successful cybersecurity career often combines certifications with substantial hands-on experience. Seek out opportunities to gain practical experience, whether through entry-level positions, internships, or even volunteering. The real-world challenges you encounter will enrich your understanding of the field, enhance your skills, and significantly improve your career prospects.

Committing to Lifelong Learning: Stay relevant in the fast-paced cybersecurity field by committing to lifelong learning. Regularly update your skills and knowledge to keep up with the latest trends, technologies, and threats. Participate in webinars, workshops, conferences, and follow industry leaders to stay informed.

In essence, a successful cybersecurity career is a blend of the right certifications, relevant experience, and a commitment to continuous learning. Set realistic career goals, understand the limitations and advantages of certifications, and prepare to embark on a lifelong learning journey. Remember, in cybersecurity, there is no final destination, only an exciting, ever-evolving path to tread.

Becoming a Certification Factory

In the quest to stand out in the cybersecurity field, there's a risk of turning into what is known as a 'Certification Factory.' This term describes the phenomenon where individuals continuously pursue certifications, stacking one on top of another, without taking time to gain and assimilate practical experience or maximize the potential of each acquired certification. While it may seem like a quick path to professional advancement, this approach often ends up being counterproductive.

Becoming a certification factory is problematic for several reasons. For one, it can result in an inability to fully integrate and apply the knowledge acquired from each certification. Certifications, while valuable, primarily provide theoretical knowledge, which needs to be supplemented by practical experience to be genuinely useful. By rapidly moving from one certification to the next, the nuanced, practical application of the knowledge gained can get lost.

Furthermore, the constant pursuit of certifications can lead to information overload, leading to an understanding that is superficial at best. Each certification is dense with complex concepts and techniques, requiring time and practice to master fully. Cramming too much information can diminish the learning efficacy, making it harder to retain and apply what was learned.

Also, the constant chase for new certifications can result in a disproportionate amount of time and money being spent on preparing for and taking exams. This approach overlooks the crucial role of on-the-job training and practical skills development, which are pivotal to a successful cybersecurity career.

To avoid becoming a certification factory, here are a few suggestions. First, consider spacing out your certifications. This strategy allows you to spend time gaining real-world experience and fully understanding the knowledge from one certification before moving onto the next.

Next, balance your theoretical knowledge with practical experience. While certifications equip you with the theory, hands-on experience solidifies that knowledge, making it more applicable in real-world scenarios.

Finally, prioritize the quality of learning over the quantity of certifications. While it's essential to keep learning and updating your skills, remember that the goal is not just to accumulate certificates but to enhance your ability to effectively perform in the cybersecurity field.

In conclusion, while certifications are valuable, turning into a certification factory can be detrimental to your long-term career growth. Instead, aim for a balanced, holistic approach to professional development in cybersecurity.

Conclusion

As we journey through the path of obtaining cybersecurity certifications, it's paramount to avoid common pitfalls and adopt strategies for success. From making an informed decision about which certification to pursue, to diligent preparation for exams, and maintaining realistic career expectations, every step is vital. Furthermore, it's important to resist the temptation to become a certification factory, constantly pursuing certificates without fully harnessing the knowledge gained or accumulating practical experience.

Ultimately, remember that the pursuit of cybersecurity certifications is a marathon, not a sprint. It demands patience, dedication, and strategic planning. By steering clear of these common mistakes, you'll be better equipped to navigate your cybersecurity career journey and reach your professional goals.

7 – Preparing "Smartly" For Certifications

Consider the story of Jane, a cybersecurity professional who decided to pursue her first certification. Jane was confident in her knowledge and experience in the field. However, she quickly realized that passing the certification exam required more than just industry experience. It required a structured study plan, effective time management, and a deep understanding of the exam structure and question types. Jane learned the hard way that mastering the art of studying and exam preparation is as crucial as understanding cybersecurity concepts themselves.

In this chapter, we aim to prevent you from falling into the same trap as Jane. We will provide you with actionable and adaptable strategies to assist you in your journey towards acing any cybersecurity certification exam. Whether you're a seasoned professional or a newcomer to the field, these strategies will help you optimize your study process and significantly enhance your chances of success.

Unlocking Success: Proven Strategies for Acing Certification Exams

Excelling in any examination, including cybersecurity certification exams, requires a robust and well-structured approach to studying. Here, we'll uncover some general, yet highly effective strategies to help you optimize your study process and set yourself up for success.

Develop a Study Schedule: It's essential to allocate dedicated time for studying to ensure consistency. Create a realistic study schedule that suits your lifestyle and preferences. Factor in breaks and leisure time to prevent burnout. As mentioned earlier, practice 'time-blocking' and set aside fixed, consistent times every day when you are most active for preparation.

Here is a sample high level plan for the CISSP if you have over 90 days to prepare.

Week	Days	Domain	Activity
1-2	1-7	Domain 1 - Security and Risk Management (15% of the exam)	Read and understand the concepts

Week	Days	Domain	Activity
1-2	8-14	Domain 1 - Security and Risk Management (15% of the exam)	Review and practice questions
3-4	15-21	Domain 2 - Asset Security (10% of the exam)	Read and understand the concepts
3-4	22-28	Domain 2 - Asset Security (10% of the exam)	Review and practice questions
5	29-32	Domain 3 - Security Architecture and Engineering (13% of the exam)	Read and understand the concepts
5	33-35	Domain 3 - Security Architecture and Engineering (13% of the exam)	Review and practice questions
6	36-39	Domain 4 - Communication and Network Security (14% of the exam)	Read and understand the concepts
6	40-42	Domain 4 - Communication and Network Security (14% of the exam)	Review and practice questions
7	43-	Domain 5 - Identity and	Read and understand the

Week	Days	Domain	Activity
	46	Access Management (13% of the exam)	concepts
7	47-49	Domain 5 - Identity and Access Management (13% of the exam)	Review and practice questions
8	50-53	Domain 6 - Security Assessment and Testing (12% of the exam)	Read and understand the concepts
8	54-56	Domain 6 - Security Assessment and Testing (12% of the exam)	Review and practice questions
9	57-60	Domain 7 - Security Operations (13% of the exam)	Read and understand the concepts
9	61-63	Domain 7 - Security Operations (13% of the exam)	Review and practice questions
10	64-67	Domain 8 - Software Development Security (10% of the exam)	Read and understand the concepts
10	68-70	Domain 8 - Software Development Security (10% of the exam)	Review and practice questions
11-12	71-80	All Domains	Review all domains, focus on weak areas
13	81-	All Domains	Take practice exams,

Week	Days	Domain	Activity
	90		review incorrect answers, and understand why you got them wrong

Set Clear Objectives: For each study session, set clear, achievable objectives. Having a specific aim helps to stay focused and prevents wasting time on irrelevant content.

Master Time Management: Time management is a crucial part of exam success. Prioritize topics based on their weight in the exam and your familiarity with them. Tackle more challenging areas when you're most alert and productive.

Take Effective Notes: Note-taking is a powerful learning tool that helps retain information and revise effectively. Develop a note-taking method that works for you - it can be bullet points, diagrams, or mind maps.

Practice Active Recall: Active recall involves actively trying to remember information rather than passively reading through notes. It's one of the most effective techniques for long-term retention of knowledge.

Embrace Spaced Repetition: It's a study technique that involves reviewing information at increasing intervals over time. This technique significantly enhances the consolidation of knowledge into long-term memory.

Leverage Practice Exams: Practice exams give a clear picture of the exam format, help improve time management, and identify areas for improvement. They also help reduce exam anxiety by familiarizing you with the exam situation.

Stay Positive: Maintaining a positive mindset can greatly influence exam performance. Believe in your capabilities, and don't let temporary setbacks deter you from your goals.

Remember, the key to success in exams is not just about the hours you put in but also about how you utilize those hours. Find what strategies work best for you, and don't be afraid to adjust your approach if something isn't working. In the following section, we will discuss how ChatGPT can aid in creating an effective study plan for your certification journey.

Using ChatGPT as your Study Partner

Now that we've covered general study strategies, let's explore how technology, specifically ChatGPT, can enhance your study process. In an age where technology is pervading every aspect of life, why not leverage it for effective studying?

Artificial intelligence, in the form of ChatGPT, can serve as a resourceful tool to help you design a comprehensive study plan. Let's dive into how you can utilize ChatGPT for your cybersecurity certification study planning.

Understanding Concepts: ChatGPT is designed to comprehend and generate text based on human-like conversation. If you're struggling to grasp a specific concept, you can ask ChatGPT to explain it in simpler terms. This can be especially beneficial for complex topics where textbook explanations may seem too complicated or jargon-filled.

For instance, if you're studying for the CISSP certification and having trouble understanding the concept of 'risk management,' you could ask, "Explain the concept of risk management in simple terms."

Creating Study Plans: ChatGPT can assist in creating a study plan tailored to your needs. Provide information about your certification, the exam date, the topics to be covered, and your available study time. ChatGPT can suggest a plan to distribute your study time efficiently.

For example, if you're planning to take the CEH exam in two months, you might ask, "How should I schedule my study time for the CEH exam in the next two months?"

A sample prompt could be:

I am preparing for the CCSK certification which is in one month. I have zero knowledge of cloud security and a full-time job. Can you propose a training plan for me. I have around an hour each day to study

Solving Queries: If you encounter doubts or questions while studying, you can use ChatGPT as a resource for clarification. It can provide explanations, examples, and even suggest further resources to explore for in-depth understanding.

For instance, if you're preparing for the AWS Certified Security exam and have a query about AWS IAM roles, you might ask, "Can you explain AWS IAM roles and their use cases?"

Reviewing Topics: ChatGPT can serve as an efficient tool for reviewing and revising learned topics. You can ask it to provide a brief overview of specific subjects or to outline key points of a topic you've studied.

For instance, if you're revising network security for the CompTIA Security+ exam, you might prompt, "Give me a brief overview of network security."

Practice Questions: Apart from explaining concepts and answering queries, ChatGPT can also generate practice questions to test your knowledge and understanding. These can be helpful to engage in active recall and gauge your preparation level.

For example, while studying for the OSCP, you might ask, "Can you generate a few practice questions related to penetration testing?"

Keep in mind that while ChatGPT is a powerful AI model capable of providing detailed and relevant responses, it's not infallible. Always cross-verify critical information from reliable sources. Furthermore, while it can help guide your study plan, you need to ensure that the plan aligns with your learning style and capacity.

By integrating tools like ChatGPT into your study strategy, you not only harness the power of AI but also make your learning experience more interactive and engaging. In the upcoming section, we will provide a summary of the key points covered in this chapter, reinforcing the valuable insights shared to help you succeed in your cybersecurity certification journey.

Chapter Summary

In this chapter, we explored strategic study techniques and how to leverage the power of AI, particularly ChatGPT, in your exam preparation process.

This chapter was designed to arm you with practical, actionable strategies to bolster your study process and improve your performance in cybersecurity certification exams. As we continue our journey, the subsequent chapters will provide further insights into enhancing your cybersecurity career, armed with the knowledge you've gained and the certifications you've achieved.

8 - A Life After Certification: What Comes Next?

Let's consider the story of Sarah, a recent graduate who had just earned her CompTIA Security+ certification. Despite her lack of extensive experience in the field, Sarah was able to land a job as a cybersecurity analyst at a reputable tech firm. How? She tailored her CV and cover letter to highlight the skills she had acquired through her certification, emphasizing her knowledge of network security and risk management. During her interview, she confidently answered questions, showcasing her certification knowledge and her passion for cybersecurity. Sarah's story is a testament to the power of effectively leveraging your certification during the job-hunting process.

This chapter shines a light on this path that lies ahead. It offers insights into the steps you need to take to leverage your certifications effectively, land that coveted cybersecurity job, and make your mark in the field. It explores various strategies to optimize your CV and LinkedIn profile, making you stand out to potential employers. It also delves into the broader possibilities, like giving back to the community, public speaking at security conferences, sharing your knowledge and insights through platforms like Medium and YouTube, and even creating your own online courses.

As we navigate through this chapter, remember that certifications are a part of your professional journey, not the destination. They are stepping stones leading you towards an enriching and rewarding cybersecurity career, filled with endless opportunities for growth and contribution. Let's get started!

Finding that Cybersecurity J-O-B

So, you've successfully completed your cybersecurity certification. Now, it's time to put that hard-earned qualification to work. Job hunting can feel overwhelming, but remember, you're not just looking for any job; you're searching for the right job where your skills, passion, and certification can shine.

When looking for a job, the first step is to identify the type of role you're interested in and the sector you want to work in. Do you want to be a network security specialist in a tech firm? Or perhaps a cybersecurity analyst in the financial sector? Define your goals.

Next, search for job postings in the cybersecurity field. Websites like LinkedIn, Indeed, and Glassdoor are excellent resources. Look for roles that match your career aspirations and pay attention to the required skills and experience. Don't be disheartened if you lack some of the 'desired' skills; job descriptions often list ideal attributes rather than strict prerequisites.

Apply to jobs that interest you, even if they seem slightly out of reach. It's common for individuals to grow into their roles. Tailor your application and cover letter to each job, highlighting your certification and how it aligns with the job requirements.

Tailoring your CV

Once you've identified potential roles, it's time to tailor your CV and cover letter to each job application. Highlight your certification prominently on your CV and discuss how the skills and knowledge you've gained align with the job requirements. Remember, your CV and cover letter are your first chance to make an impression, so ensure they're concise, error-free, and compelling.

When crafting your CV, focus on the following:

1. Highlight your cybersecurity certification: Mention it early in your CV, either in your summary or in a dedicated 'Certifications' section.
2. Showcase relevant skills: List the skills you've gained through your certification that align with the job requirements. Be specific and, where possible, provide examples of how you've applied these skills.
3. Include any relevant experience: If you've had practical experience, such as internships, projects, or volunteer work, be sure to include it. Describe what you did and what you learned.

In your cover letter, tell a story. Explain why you're interested in the role and how your certification has prepared you for it. Show enthusiasm and commitment, and make it clear why you'd be a great fit for the position.

Next, prepare for the job interview. Research common cybersecurity interview questions and practice your answers. Questions may range from technical queries, like explaining how a VPN works, to situational questions, such as how you would handle a security breach. Be ready to discuss your certification and how the skills you've gained make you a strong candidate.

Remember, job descriptions often list ideal attributes rather than strict prerequisites. Don't be disheartened if you lack some of the 'desired' skills. Apply to jobs that interest you, even if they seem slightly out of reach. It's common for individuals to grow into their roles.

Finally, while job hunting can sometimes feel like a waiting game, remember that you're not just looking for any job; you're searching for the right job where your skills, passion, and certification can shine. Stay patient, persistent, and positive, and you'll find the right opportunity."

Improving Your LinkedIn

Also remember that when it comes to finding jobs there are two ways:

- Going to where the jobs are
- Making the jobs come to you

The first is the tried and tested way of going to the job i.e., find a job that you like, apply with your CV / LinkedIn and wait for the response. There is nothing wrong with that approach and how most people find their jobs however there is the issue of just passively waiting for something to happen

The other approach is to make the jobs come to you i.e., make your cyber security profile a job magnet so that recruiters seek you out and approach you for that next high-paying job

The best way to do that is to improve your LinkedIn Profile and there is a reason that improving your LinkedIn is almost universal advice given for increasing your chances of getting a better-paying job

LinkedIn IS the new CV and the place where most recruiters find you if they are looking for your skillset

If your LinkedIn is drab and boring, then you are greatly reducing your chances of being discovered no matter how strong your cyber-security knowledge is

Apart from the general stuff like putting in your certifications and job title, there are some tips you should keep in mind

Use the LinkedIn banner image and Headline to grab attention. The profile below immediately tells a recruiter where a person works PLUS what the areas of specialties are

Taimur Ijlal
Cloud Security Pro | 🖥 A.I. Noob | ✍ Writer | 🇬🇧 UK Global
Talent VISA holder

Take full advantage of the "Featured" section on your LinkedIn profile. This is the best place to showcase your achievements and awards you might have won. Also, any good articles you might have written, videos etc.

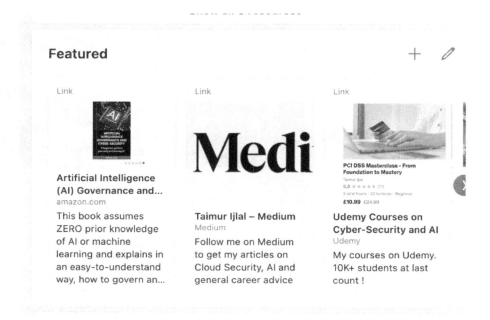

When putting in details of your current job experience; do not just put in your job description and what you do but put in the achievements also. The extra stuff you did to stand out in your current position. Remember that the hiring manager is interested in what unique strengths you are bringing to the table and not just what your 9–5 duties are!

Use the media section for each job to add any awards or conferences you attended while in this position.

How to Stand out in the Industry

No one will reach out to hire you if no one knows you ! Aside from job-hunting, there are other ways to brand yourself and establish yourself as an authority in the field. Here are a few ways you can increase your reach and network with other professionals.

1 - Conferences, Mentorships and Seminars

Beyond finding a job, being a part of the cybersecurity community involves more than just work. It's about contributing to the collective knowledge, aiding in the growth and development of others, and helping to make the digital world a safer place.

Consider volunteering your skills for non-profit organizations or open-source projects. Many such groups are in need of cybersecurity expertise but cannot afford professional consultation. This is not only rewarding on a personal level but can also provide you with additional hands-on experience to complement your certification.

Another way to give back is through mentorship. If you've been in the cybersecurity field for a while, you can guide others who are just starting. Sharing your experience and knowledge can be highly rewarding and also helps to build a stronger, more informed community.

Public speaking is another excellent way to contribute to the cybersecurity community, and it's a chance to demonstrate your knowledge, share insights, and network with industry peers. Consider submitting a proposal to speak at security conferences. These events typically welcome new speakers and fresh perspectives on cybersecurity topics. Your recent completion of a cybersecurity certification can bring unique insights to the table.

When preparing a speech or presentation, consider what you've learned in your certification process that would be valuable to others. Are there emerging trends that need more attention? Can you offer a new perspective on a contentious issue? Or perhaps you can share practical advice or lessons learned from your experience.

Remember, public speaking doesn't mean you have to be an expert on every aspect of cybersecurity. It's about sharing what you know and fostering conversations around those topics. Your authenticity and passion can inspire and motivate others in the field.

Public speaking enhances your professional brand. It can make you more visible to potential employers, open doors to new opportunities, and position you as a thought leader in your area of expertise. It's a valuable skill that can complement your cybersecurity certification and enhance your career progression.

2 - Writing on Medium

The vast realm of cybersecurity can often seem daunting to outsiders and newcomers, which makes it all the more crucial for professionals in the field to share their knowledge, insights, and experiences. Medium, an online platform that emphasizes insightful and thought-provoking content, provides an excellent opportunity to do just that

. By writing about your journey, the challenges you've faced, the certifications you've earned, and the knowledge you've gained, you can demystify the field for those considering a career in cybersecurity. Furthermore, your posts can also serve as a valuable resource for your peers in the industry.

Writing on Medium also benefits you by establishing your reputation as a knowledgeable professional in your field. As you consistently publish insightful content, you'll likely garner a following of readers who appreciate your expertise and perspective. This can lead to networking opportunities and even job offers.

Here are some strategies to help you succeed:

1. Consistency is Key: Regularly publish articles to keep your readers engaged and coming back for more. Aim to publish at least once a week.
2. Quality Over Quantity: While it's important to publish consistently, don't sacrifice quality for quantity. Well-researched, insightful articles will attract more readers and followers.
3. Engage with Your Readers: Respond to comments on your articles to foster a sense of community. Engaging with your readers can lead to interesting discussions and can also give you ideas for future articles.
4. Leverage SEO: Use relevant keywords in your article title and throughout your content to make it more discoverable.
5. Promote Your Articles: Share your articles on your social media platforms and relevant online communities to reach a wider audience.

3 - Creating YouTube Shorts or Videos

Creating educational YouTube content is another highly effective way to share your knowledge, build your brand, and potentially diversify your income. Cybersecurity is a field that is rich in technical depth, making it ideal for informative video content. You can create comprehensive tutorials, share insights about current cybersecurity trends, provide tips for passing specific certification exams, or even share stories about your career journey.

YouTube's format allows for a much more dynamic and engaging approach than written content. You can utilize visual aids, animations, screen recordings, and even incorporate hands-on demonstrations to convey complex concepts effectively. YouTube Shorts, brief 60-second videos, are an excellent way to share bite-sized tips and insights, and they can serve as a way to attract viewers to your longer, more detailed content.

Moreover, the growing demand for cybersecurity professionals means there is a significant audience looking for guidance and education in the field. Your YouTube channel can become a valuable resource for these individuals. As your channel grows, so too will your influence and credibility within the cybersecurity industry.

Here are some tips to help you succeed:

1. Consistent Posting: Similar to Medium, consistency is crucial on YouTube. Aim to post new videos regularly to keep your audience engaged.
2. Quality Content: Ensure your videos are high-quality, both in terms of the content and the production. Clear audio, good lighting, and engaging visuals can make a significant difference in attracting and retaining viewers.
3. SEO Matters: Use relevant keywords in your video titles, descriptions, and tags to make your videos more discoverable.
4. Engage with Your Audience: Encourage viewers to like, comment, and subscribe, and make sure to respond to comments to foster a sense of community.
5. Leverage YouTube Shorts: YouTube Shorts are a great way to share bite-sized tips and insights. They can serve as a way to attract viewers to your longer, more detailed content.

The Way Forward

As we conclude this chapter, let's reflect on the story of Lisa, a cybersecurity professional who used her certifications as stepping stones in her career. After earning her certifications,

Lisa didn't stop there. She actively sought out opportunities to apply her skills, landing a job that allowed her to grow and learn. She also contributed to the cybersecurity community, speaking at conferences, and even mentoring others. Lisa understood that her certifications were part of her journey, not the destination. She embodies the spirit of continuous learning and growth that is crucial in the cybersecurity field. As you move forward in your own journey, remember Lisa's story. Use your certifications as she did - as tools to open doors, contribute to the community, and continue learning and growing

Now, it's time for you to take the next step. Whether that's applying for jobs, optimizing your LinkedIn profile, writing your first Medium article, or filming your first YouTube video, don't hesitate. The cybersecurity field needs your unique skills and insights. So, keep learning, keep sharing, and keep growing. Your journey in cybersecurity has just begun, and the possibilities are endless.

9 – Your Certification Journey Awaits

Congratulations on reaching the end of this book and hopefully now have a good view on your cybersecurity certification path and where you want to go in your career.

This is just the start of your journey as Cybersecurity is a massive field with new niches emerging regularly.

Before you go, I want to leave you with a few key points:

- Remember that Practical Experience is crucial ! Certifications can demonstrate theoretical knowledge, but cybersecurity is a hands-on field. It's about outthinking attackers, problem-solving on the fly, and being prepared for the unexpected. These skills are honed through experience, not exams.

- Depth Over Breadth: While it's great to have a wide knowledge base, the cybersecurity world also values deep expertise. Chasing every certification can result in a jack-of-all-trades, master-of-none situation. Consider focusing on specific areas to become a sought-after expert.
- Apply What You Learn: Try to gain practical experience where you can apply your knowledge. This could be in your current job, an internship, a new role, or even simulated environments.

Get in touch

Feel free to get in touch with me via the below. Always happy to hear from my readers!

YouTube: https://www.youtube.com/@CloudSecurityGuy
Medium: https://medium.com/@taimurcloud123
Newsletter: https://cloudsecurityguy.substack.com/
LinkedIn: https://www.linkedin.com/in/taimurijlal/

Feedback time

I would **really** appreciate you leaving me a quick review on Amazon and feedback will help me to further improve this book and grow as a writer. It only takes a few minutes, and I would be extremely grateful for the same

I wish you all the best in your AI security journey!

.

ABOUT THE AUTHOR

Taimur Ijlal is a multi-award-winning information security leader with over two decades of international experience in cyber-security and IT risk management in the fin-tech industry. For his contributions to the industry, he won a few awards here and there, such as CISO of the Year, CISO Top 30, CISO Top 50, and Most Outstanding Security Team.

He served as the Head of Information Security for several major companies, but his real passion is teaching and writing about cyber-security topics. He lives in the UK, where he moved with his family in 2021.

Taimur writes on Medium and has a YouTube channel, "Cloud Security Guy, " where he regularly posts about Cloud Security, Artificial Intelligence, and general cyber-security career advice.

He has published two books on AI Cybersecurity and Zero Trust, both of which can be purchased from Amazon. He also has several courses on Udemy and can be contacted on his LinkedIn profile for any consulting opportunities.

Made in the USA
Las Vegas, NV
26 November 2023

81579509R00072